"Enhancement of CodeCover Tool for JAVA Projects"

ACKNOWLEDGEMENT

I thank Mr. **Rainer** of Stuttgart University for his help during setting up of the code base.

I thank all my **Family members** without whose support this work would not have been completed.

Abhinandan H. Patil

Contents

List of Figures

ACRONYMS

Abbreviation	Description
API	Application Programming Interface
BC	Branch Coverage
BCEL	Byte Code Engineering Library
CFG	Control Flow Graph
CLI	Command Line Interface
CSV	Comma Separated Values
CUT	Code Under Test
EPL	Eclipse Public License
HTML	Hyper Text Markup Language
IDE	Integrated Development Environment
JDK	Java Development Kit
JRE	Java Runtime Environment
JVM	Java Virtual Machine
OS	Operating System
SC	Statement Coverage
SDLC	Software Development Life Cycle
SRS	System Requirement Specification
SVN	Sub Version
SWT	Standard Widget ToolKit
UI	User Interface
UML	Unified Modeling Language
XML	eXtensive Markup Language

Chapter 1 INTRODUCTION

1.1 Introduction to Code Coverage Tools.

Software testing is an essential activity for program validation. Exhaustive testing is not possible all the time; next option is adequate testing which is performed by obtaining the test model of code under test (CUT) at different level of abstraction. Control flow graph (CFG) based coverage testing for structural entities (e.g. statements in the code) are among the most popular testing techniques used in practice.

Code keeps on changing because of frequent activities such as bug fixes, code re-factoring and software upgrades. The purpose of regression testing is to ensure that these changes in the code do not adversely affect the correct functionality inherited from its previous version. Test suite augmentation is the process in which new test cases are added to uncover bugs introduced by new code/modified code. Test case prioritization is an approach of ordering the test cases in terms of some effectiveness criteria which can be used further for other activities like enhancing regression testing, test suite minimization, etc. There are various approaches for test case prioritization, many of which make use of coverage information.

Code coverage analysis is the process of finding areas of a program not exercised by a set of test cases, thereby resulting in a quantitative measure of code coverage, which is an indirect measure of code quality. At the same time it can help in creating additional test cases to increase the coverage and may identify unreachable portions of the code. Additionally, it can identify redundant test cases that do not increase coverage, as well as help in testing changes made to the code during regression testing. A proper coverage tool is highly desirable to meet all these requirements.

Coverage measures based on various code-elements such as methods, statements, blocks, branches and predicates are most widely employed for coverage based testing. The coverage analysis tools are language dependent. Coverage analyzers introduce probes which increment counters. This process is called instrumentation. Java coverage analyzers can be classified on the basis of instrumentation as:

- Source code instrumentation
- Bytecode instrumentation
- Those that run the code in a modified JVM.

Bytecode instrumentation adds probe instructions directly to the bytecode. It is very useful in situations where the source code is not available. Bytecode instrumentation neither requires modified JVM nor requires recompiling of source code second time. It can provide integral coverage for single statement at source code level (a source code line may contain multiple code statements) and can be easily integrated to run on the fly.

Study of CodeCover and JavaCodeCover was carried out and the following advantages of CodeCover were identified over JavaCodeCover:

- CodeCover is an extensible open source code coverage tool.
- Supports statement coverage, branch coverage, loop coverage and strict condition coverage (aka condition/decision coverage).
- Performs source instrumentation for the most accurate coverage measurement.
- Provides CLI interface, for easy use from the command line.
- Provides Ant interface, for easy integration into an existing build process.
- Is completely integrated into Eclipse.
- Generates customizable HTML and CSV report.
- Per test case coverage measurement.
- Totally integrated with JUnit for automatic recognition of test cases.
- Boolean Analyzer feature is present which helps to find test cases to increase strict condition coverage.

- Correlation Matrix feature is present which helps to find redundant test cases and test suite optimization.

The task at hand involves doing reverse engineering of the product and enhancing the CodeCover Tool.

1.2 CodeCover Tool Basics

Testing is the process of executing program with the intent of finding bugs. During glass box testing, the execution of code element is recorded. The code element can be either statement, branch, condition or loop. The complete program element set is known and finite. Glass box testing is same as white box testing which in other words is called as coverage testing. Test coverage is the degree to which the complete sets of program elements are recorded. A test case consists of execution of conditions, input data and expected results. A test suite is set of test cases.

Functional Testing involves three steps viz. Test case creation, Test execution and Test reporting. On the basis of the specification of System under Test (SUT), test cases and hence test suite are created. The test cases are executed with the SUT and expected results and actual results are compared. The verdict whether the test case passed or failed depends upon this comparison.

The Benefits of Glass Box Testing are as follows

1. Testing adequacy metric

Coverage is an objective testing adequacy metric which can be used as completion criterion for testing. If the coverage is adequate, the probability that the test cases have exercised the code is more and vice versa.

2. Test suite extension

The glass box test denotes the program elements that are not executed. This data can be utilized for the test suite extension.

3. Test suite reduction

Removing (redundant) test cases from a test suite to reduce regression testing effort without (significantly) decreasing testing effectiveness

4. Basis for selective regression testing

Instead of running all the test cases only those that are involved in the code modification can be executed.

5. Support for program comprehension

The traceability is provided in the form of which test case executed which part of the code.

1.3 Issues and Challenges

Myriad tools are available to get the code coverage report of the projects as depicted in the comparison table of code coverage tools. At present all the available tools are mere data generation/presentation tools which will give the measure of coverage of the testing activity.

There is ever growing demand for incorporating intelligence in Tools by which the Tools could suggest the measures to increase the coverage and hence effectiveness of testing.

This project attempts to show ways to incorporate intelligence in the Tool by which the Tool will be enhanced from mere data generation/presentation Tool to quality enhancement Tool.

1.4   Problem Statement

Unit testing drives the code quality and code coverage Tool drives code coverage, the unit testing improvement is achievable by enhancing the existing code coverage Tools.

The chosen code coverage Tool should be open source software which will run on various platforms such as Windows, Linux and Mac OS. Further, the Tool should be extensible for non Java projects as well.

The enhancements can be achieved by doing reverse engineering of the existing code base and coming up with intelligence incorporation by which the Tool will start suggesting the test cases to be added for increasing the coverage.

There is need for paradigm shift from data generation/presentation to strengthening of the quality of the product.

1.5 Aim and Objective

The aims and objectives of the project are as follows:

- Generation of new matrices to strengthen the code coverage and hence the quality.

- Incorporating intelligence in the tool by which the paradigm is shifted from data generation/presentation to test suite enhancement.

- Generation of new matrices for strengthening the test suite

- Enhancement of Eclipse interface.

- Highlighting of the vulnerable areas of the quality process being followed in the project.

Chapter 2 LITERATURE SURVEY

Literature survey is the most important phase in software development process. In this phase a study of existing work was carried and deep thought was given to what is to be incorporated by going through several papers presented in various forums. The survey involves studying of the capability of the existing Tools available in the market place both open source and proprietary. Post literature survey it was evident as to what should be incorporated in the tool and possible impact of the enhancement of the Tool on the product employing the Tool.

2.1 Previous Research work

The topic code coverage has been studied exhaustively [23-28]. Many tools are readily available off the shelf (both proprietary and open source) for coverage analysis of Java. This project studies a tool called CodeCover and mentions about features and highlights the ease with which enhancements can be incorporated in the tool for particular needs.

Testing drives the code quality and code coverage is vital entity of testing. Since bug fixes, code-refactoring and software enhancement activities are frequently carried out in life cycle of the product there is the need for testing activity as well. Since it is desirable to know the quantitative effectiveness of testing one takes solace in code coverage metrics.

Depending upon the nature of testing viz. unit testing, component testing or regression testing the nature of support expected from the tool differs. CodeCover supports command line, Ant integration and Eclipse plug in modes for these needs.

Further, CodeCover makes use of source code instrumentation for accurate results when compared to Byte code instrumentation.

The next step after decision to gather coverage metrics is choice of the tool. There are proprietary tools [8] which cost as much as $2200 for 10 machine license. CodeCover [1] is freely available tool with support and comes with EPL licensing agreement. The code can be freely downloaded, extended, tweaked as per the specific needs. The documentation is available

[2] for CodeCover. The references [31, 32, 34 and 36] give additional information on the usage of CodeCover.

There are other open source code coverage tools such as cobertura[3] which are yet to be updated for the latest version of Java (As of this writing). The Tool such as Emma [4] offer subset of the functionality offered by CodeCover (Eclipse support is missing). Tools such as Eclemma are tightly coupled with Eclipse environment hence may not be suited for legacy projects. The tools such as JavaCodeCoverage[6] offer only minimal subset functionality of functionality of CodeCover. Moreover, although such tools are termed as OpenSource tools [11], the code is not available anywhere on the net and such tools are coupled with particular operating system. Considering the facts listed above this paper decided to finalize on CodeCover.

The focus area in large projects has been Regression Test Suite Maintenance. H. Agarwal et al. [12] focused on Incremental regression testing. Since it is not possible to run all the test cases of Regression considering the resource constraints, S. Elabaum et al. [13] proposed Test case prioritization. M. J. Harold et al. proposed Regression test selection for Java projects. Test suite reduction and prioritization has been focus for J. A. Jones et al [15]. The other area of research has been open code coverage framework supporting multiple languages by Sakamoto. K. et al [22]. Code coverage has been main focus of the several papers [23-28]. Although there are many papers published for the code coverage, few papers are there on particular code coverage tool. This paper therefore focuses on particular code coverage tool for Java projects and intends to aid the Testers, Developers and Code Coverage tool developers in zeroing on code coverage tool.

The Code Coverage analysis is the testing activity (May be part of Unit Testing, Component Testing, Regression Testing), where in uncovered (untested) code is highlighted. The metrics give the quantitative measure of tested code and untested code.

The chapter on Structural testing of the text book by Mauro pezze and Michal young [29] gives the various parameters of interest during the code coverage. Code coverage is measure of code quality [23-28]. Various parameters collected during code coverage analysis can be used for multiple purposes.

Test suite is another area of study which is studied exhaustively in several papers [14, 15, 17].Test suite prioritization work is carried out in few papers [18]. Junit test case development study is area of focus for few papers [37, 33].Van Rompey et al talk about estimation of test code changes using historical data [40].Del Frate et al correlate the code coverage and software reliability[28,46].Li J.J et al talk about relating testing of software design specification[39].

The code coverage tools are classified into three main categories on the basis of instrumentation technique followed:

Source code instrumenting tools, Byte code instrumenting tools (often making use of BCEL [7]) and those that run the code in modified JVM. The source code instrumentation and byte code instrumentation tools are widely used. Source code instrumentation tools add probe in the modified source code.

2.2 Existing System and Its Effect

The CodeCover Tool gives the options to gather the coverage data when run in command-line, Ant integration mode and Eclipse environment.

When run in Eclipse mode, codecover gives the various views with specific functionality. However, no Tools including CodeCover give the view which will recommend measures to strengthen the Quality.

2.3 Proposed System and Its advantage

This project proposes introduction of new features in to the system of CodeCover by which the Tool will intelligently start suggesting the test cases for strengthening the test suite. The tool will start suggesting areas which are vulnerable and hence need attention.

The test suite can be enhanced in-line with the suggestion of the CodeCover post enhancement to plug the loop holes in the Test suite.

The proposed advantage is improved code quality.

Chapter 3 SOFTWARE REQUIREMENT SPECIFICATON

A Software Requirements Specification (SRS) is a complete description of the behavior of the system to be developed. It includes the functional and non functional requirement for the software to be developed. The functional requirement includes what the software should do and non functional requirement define how the system is supposed to be. Requirements must be measurable, testable, related to identified needs or opportunities, and defined to a level of detail sufficient for system design.

What the software has to do is directly perceived by its users – either human users or other software systems. The common understanding between the user and developer is captured in requirements document. The writing of software requirement specification reduces development effort, as careful review of the document can reveal omissions, misunderstandings, and inconsistencies early in the development cycle when these problems are easier to correct. The SRS discusses the product but not the project that developed it; hence the SRS serves as a basis for later enhancement of the finished product. The SRS may need to be altered, but it does provide a foundation for continued production evaluation.

3.1   Overall Description

This section provides a description of the general factors that affect the product and its requirements. It also deals with user characteristics, constraints on using the product and dependencies of the product on other applications.

3.1.1 Product Perspective

The Code Cover Tool is basically designed for gathering/reporting of vital parameters of Code Coverage. The proposed enhancement should provide additional parameters which will be used by the quality personnel to strengthen the testing further. The System being developed should be user friendly and reliable software for the above purpose.

3.1.2 Product Functions

The primary function of the product is to gather the coverage data for testing. With the proposed enhancements the Tool will start suggesting test cases at the method level for increasing the coverage. The Tool shall highlight the vulnerable areas of the quality process and hence recommend for prioritizing the test cases. It should be usable in real time projects and should be flexible enough to run on various platforms viz. Windows and Linux platforms.

3.1.3 User Characteristics

This section tells what the expected user characteristics are:

- To use the application the user must know the key terminologies used with Coverage.
- User has the necessary resources in the form of software/hardware as outlined in the subsequent sections.

3.1.4 Pre-requisites

- The user should have installed one of the operating system viz. Windows, Linux or Mac on one of the systems with hardware specification as mentioned in the subsequent section.
- The product is being developed using java language so user platform should have Java Runtime Environment (JRE) to run this application.
- The user should have the Apache Ant installed on the host to run the Tool in Ant Integration mode.
- User should have intelligent xml editors such as XML copy editor installed on the host being used for the testing.

3.1.5 Assumptions and Dependencies

This section tells what are the assumptions and dependencies.
- The product accepts external intelligence through the XML files in such cases the User should have the relevant data to feed to the Tool.

3.2   Specific Requirements

This section of the SRS should contain all the software requirements to a level of detail sufficient to enable designers to design a system to satisfy those requirements. It also helps tester to design their test case to verify whether system satisfies the specified requirements.

3.2.1 Functional Requirement

The CodeCover shall instrument the application under scrutiny and shall generate all the necessary vital parameters of interest to the quality team. Further, the tool shall generate the data which will help in prioritizing the test suite or pruning of the Test suite. The tool shall have the functionality where in external data could be fed to the Tool in the form of XML files.

3.2.2 Non Functional Requirement

- **Usability:** The Tool should be usable for real time projects.
- **User Friendly:** The documents should be available in the form of tutorial and manuals for ease of usage of the Tool.
- **Maintainability:** The product being developed should be maintainable. Design documents, proper code comments, coding guidelines etc should be followed while developing any additional software.
- **Availability:** System should be available whenever the project wants to gather the coverage reports.
- **Portability:** The application is developed in Java. It would be portable to other operating system provided JDK is available for the OS.
- **Extensibility**: The project work should be open for any future modification and hence the work could be defined as the one of the extensible work.

3.2.3 Software Requirement
The software requirements are listed below:
- **Operating System**   : Windows or Linux or Mac.
- **Programming Language** : Java Programming

- **Front end** : Swings
- **Tools used** : Eclipse as Integrated Development Environment, SubVersion for getting the code base, Ant for building the project.ESS for Reverse Engineering, Violet for UML Diagrams, XML Copy Editor for editing the XML files.

3.2.4 Hardware Requirement

- **Processor** : Pentium IV 2.5 GHz
- **Memory** : 512 MB of RAM, 1 GB recommended.
- **Hard disk** : 1 GB Hard Disk.
- **Display** : 1024 X 768 or higher resolution display with 16 bit color.

3.2.5 Performance Requirements

- **Response Time:** The time taken by Tool to instrument the source code gather/report the data should be less than 1 minutes (60 Seconds).

3.2.6 Resource Requirements

The development makes use of Standard Widget Tool Kit for developing the interface.SWT is open source software. The development in Eclipse for providing a graphical user interface (GUI) for Java programs is through SWT. SWT was developed to provide a more sophisticated set of GUI components than the earlier Abstract Window Toolkit. SWT provides a native look and feel that emulates the look and feel of several platforms, and also supports a pluggable look and feel that allows applications to have a look and feel unrelated to the underlying platform.

The software developed using SWT possess the following characteristics.

- **Extensibility**: The applications developed using SWT are highly extensible.
- **Platform Independence:** The SWT abstracts out the User Interface (UI) details of a given operating system in the SWT layer.

- **Component-oriented:** SWT is a component-based framework.

- **Customizable:** The UI developed will be customizable.

- **Configurable:** The UI will be configurable.

- **Lightweight UI**: The UI will be lightweight.

- **Look and Feel:** SWT allows one to specialize the look and feel of widgets.

3.2.7 Eclipse

Eclipse refers to both a platform framework for Java desktop applications, and an integrated development environment (IDE) for developing with Java and much more (for a complete overview visit the website of Eclipse). The Eclipse IDE is written in Java and runs everywhere where a JVM is installed, including Windows, Mac OS, Linux, and Solaris. A JDK is required for Java development functionality, but is not required for development in other programming languages. The Eclipse Platform allows applications to be developed from a set of modular software components called *projects*. Applications based on the Eclipse platform (including the Eclipse IDE) can be extended by third party developers

Chapter 4 SYSTEM ANALYSIS

Analysis involves a detailed study of the current system, leading to specifications of a new system. Analysis is a detailed study of various operations performed by a system and their relationships within and outside the system. All procedures, requirements must be analyzed and documented. System analysis also includes sub-dividing of complex process involving the entire system.

4.1   Defining a System

A collection of components that work together to realize some objectives forms a system. Basically there are three major components in every system, namely input, processing and output.

In a system the different components are connected with each other and they are interdependent. The objective of the system demands that some output is produced as a result of processing the suitable inputs.

4.2   System Life Cycle

System life cycle is an organizational process of developing and maintaining systems. It helps in establishing a system project plan, because it gives overall list of processes and sub-processes required developing a system.

System development life cycle means combination of various activities. In other words they can say that various activities put together are referred as system development life cycle. In the system analysis and design terminology, the system development life cycle means software development life cycle.

Following are the different phases of software development cycle:

- System study
- Feasibility study
- System analysis
- System design
- Coding

- Testing
- Implementation
- Maintenance

4.3   Phases of System Development Life Cycle

Let us now describe the different phases and the related activities of system development life cycle in detail.

4.3.1 System Study

System study is the first stage of the system development life cycle. This gives a clear picture of what actually the physical system is. In practice, the system study is done in two phases .In first phase, the primary survey of the system is done which helps in identifying the scope of the system.

The second phase of the system study is more detailed and in-depth study in which the identification of user' requirement and the limitations and problems of the present system are studied. After completing the system study, a system proposal is prepared by the System Analyst (who studies the system) and placed before the user. The proposed system contains the findings of the present system and recommendations to overcome the limitations and problems of the present system in the light of the user's requirements.

In this phase the existing code base of CodeCover was downloaded and it was reverse engineered. The existing code base was studied with the intention of mapping existing code to the implicit/explicit requirements of the Tool.

The planned Enhancements are studied are studied in this phase. The outcome of this phase is comparison of Existing System vis-à-vis Planned System.

4.3.2 Feasibility Study

On the basis of the results of the initial study, feasibility study was done. Study was done basically to implement the proposed system in the light of its workability, meeting user's requirements, effective use of resources and of course the cost effectiveness.

By extrapolating the data already available for the existing functionality (which was collected using Metrics plug-in of Eclipse), it was inferred that the Enhancements are implementable in the time line available for project.

Following feasibility study was done:

- **Technical feasibility:** The project is technically feasible as the intended functionality is extension of the existing functionality with modifications. The guestimates of project show that it is implementable in the given time line.

- **Economical Feasibility:** The economical feasibility must satisfy the needs of the technical feasibility and the operational feasibility. It involves the economic feasibility of developing and implementing the proposed system. This is developed with minimum cost and it will perform all possible task needed by user, similar to the existing system.

- **Operational Feasibility:** Operational Feasibility supports all the user environments and solves the user's needs.

4.3.3 System Analysis

Assuming that the system is to be developed, the next, phase is system analysis. Analysis involved a detailed study of the current system, leading to specifications of a new system.

4.3.4 System Design

Based on the user requirements and the detailed design analysis of a new system, the new system must be designed. This is the phase of system designing. It is a most crucial phase in the development of a system. Normally, the design proceeds in two stages:

- Preliminary or general design
- Structure or detailed design

In the preliminary or general design, the features of the new system are specified. The costs of implementing these features and the benefits to be derived are estimated. If the project is still considered to be feasible, the next step is detailed design.

In the detailed design stage, computer oriented work begins. At this stage, the design of the system becomes more structured. Structure design is a blue print of a computer system solution to a given problem having the same components and inter-relationship among the same components as the original problem. Input, output and processing specifications are drawn up in detail. In the design stage, the programming language and the platform in which the new system will run are also decided.

4.3.5 Coding

After designing the new system, the whole system is required to be converted into computer understanding language. Coding the new system into computer programming language does this. It is an important stage where the defined procedures are transformed into control specifications by the help of computer language. This is also called the programming phase in which the programmer converts the program specifications into computer instructions, which are referred as programs. The programs coordinate the data movements and control the entire process in a system. It is generally felt that the program must be modular in nature. This helps in the fast development, maintenance and future change, if required.

4.3.6 Testing

 Before actually implementing the new system into operations, a test run of the system is done to remove all the bugs, if any. After codifying the whole programs of the system, test plan should be developed and run on a given set of test data. The output of the test run should match the expected results.

Using the test data following test run are carried out:

- Unit test
- System test

Unit test: when the programs have been coded and compiled and brought to working conditions, they must be individually tested with the prepared test data. Any undesirable happening must be noted and debugged (error corrections).

System test: After carrying out the unit testing for each of the program of the system and when errors are removed, then system test is done. At this stage the test is done on the actual data. The complete system is executed on the actual data. At each stage of execution, the results or the output is analyzed. During the result analysis, it may be found that the outputs are not matching the expected out of the system. In such case, the errors in the particular programs are identified that the system is running error-free, the users are called with their own actual data so that the system could be shown running as per their requirements.

4.3.7 Implementation

After having the user acceptance of the new system developed, the implementation phase begins. Implementation is the stage of a project during which theory is turned into practice. Implementation is planned in two phase high level design and low level design. The project uses the Violet software for UML Diagrams and coding is done with Java in Eclipse IDE.

4.3.8 Maintenance

Maintenance is necessary to eliminate errors in the system during its working life and to tune the system to any variations in its working environment. It has been seen that there are always some errors found in the system that must be noted and corrected. It also means the review of the system from time to time. The review of the system is done for:

- Knowing the full capabilities of the system.
- Knowing the required changes or the additional requirements.
- Studying the performance.

Chapter 5 SYSTEM DESIGN

The purpose of the design is to plan the solution of a problem specified by the requirement specification. This phase is the first step in moving from problem to the solution domain. The design of the system is perhaps the most critical factor affecting the quality of the software and has a major impact on the later phases, particularly testing and maintenance. System design aims to identify the modules that should be in the system, the specifications of these modules to interact with each other to produce the desired results. At the end of the system design all the major data structures, file formats, output formats as well as major modules in the system and their specifications are decided.

5.1   Design Considerations

This section describes many of the issues which are needed to be addressed or resolved before attempting to devise a complete design solution.

5.2   Development Method

The project work is using the waterfall lifecycle model for the development of the project. The waterfall model is an activity centered lifecycle model.

The approach of the waterfall model is in a step-by-step way where all the requirements of one activity are completed before the design of the activity is started. The entire project design is broken down into several small tasks in order of precedence and these tasks are designed one by one making sure they work perfectly. Once one of these small tasks is completed another task, which is dependent on the completed task, can be started. Each step after being completed is verified to ensure the task is working, error-free and meeting all the requirements.

The project work chose this lifecycle model for the project primarily for two reasons. First reason being simplicity, by using the waterfall model the entire project can be broken down into smaller activities which can be converted relatively easily into code and once the entire thing is combined the code for the project can be derived. The second reason is because of the verification step required by the waterfall model it would be ensured that a task is error free before other tasks that are dependent on it are developed. Thus chances of an error remaining somewhere high up in the task hierarchy are relatively low.

Some of the unique features of waterfall model are:

- It can be implemented for all size projects.

- It leads to a concrete and clear approach to software development.

- In this model testing is inherent in every phase.

- Documentation is produced at every stage of model which is very helpful for people who are involved.

Schematic illustration of waterfall model:

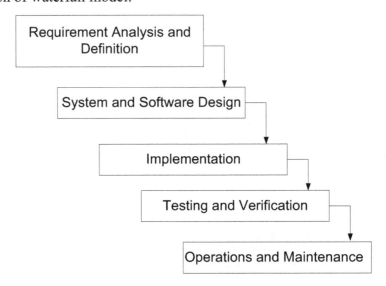

Figure 1. Schematic Illustration of WaterFall Model

The model consists of following distinct stages, namely:

- Requirement Analysis & Definition: In this stage the problem is specified along with the desired service objectives (goals) and the constraints are identified. In this phase the requirements were gathered for the enhancement project of CodeCover.

- System & Software Design: In this stage the system specifications are translated into a software representation. The software engineer at this stage is concerned with data structure, software architecture and interface representations. In this phase CodeCover System and Software Design was carried out. The system architecture was decided and Class Diagrams and Sequence Diagrams were drawn.

- Implementation: In this stage the designs are translated into the software domain. In this phase the actual coding of the project was done.

- Unit, Integration & System Testing: Testing at this stage focuses on making sure that any errors are identified and that the software meets its required specification. After this stage the software is delivered to the customer. In this phase the Unit, Integration and System testing were carried out.

- Operations & Maintenance: In this phase the software is updated to meet the changing customer needs, adapted to accommodate changes in the external environment, correct errors and oversights previously undetected in the testing phases, enhancing the efficiency of the software. This is the last phase employed by CodeCover enhancement project.

5.3   System Architecture

Large systems are always decomposed into sub-systems that provide some related set of services. The initial design process of identifying these sub-systems and establishing a framework for sub-system control and communication is called architecture design and the output of this design process is a description of the software architecture.

The architectural design process is concerned with establishing a basic structural framework for a system. It involves identifying the major components of the system and communications between these components. In the following sub-sections we delve into the design aspects and the sub systems involved in this software package.

5.3.1 System Overview

The system overview provides the actual view of the application in the real time environment. Below figure shows the system overview. As depicted in the figure the application is top most layer of the design which interacts with the Recommendation Generator. Recommendation Generator interacts with the coverage generator for acquiring the required data. The Eclipse GUI is the lowest layer which provides the required data for the coverage generator

5.4   Use Case Diagrams

A use case is a set of scenarios that describing an interaction between a user and a system. The main purpose of a use case diagram is to show what system functions are performed for which actor they do not make any attempt to represent the order or number of times that the systems actions and sub-actions should be executed. The actor sets up the environment for CodeCover. The CodeCover is plugged into the Eclipse environment. User populates the input data with the help of XMLs and the code coverage data is gathered. With the help of generated code coverage data, the recommendation generator provides the recommendation data. Finally user can export the data to Excel sheet if desired.

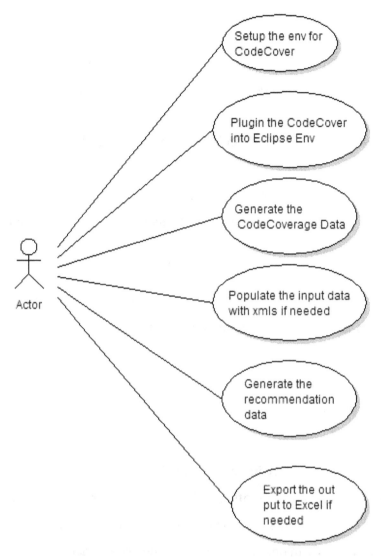

Figure 2. Use Case Diagrams

5.5   Sequence Diagrams

A sequence diagram shows how processes operate with one another and in what order. It is a construct of a Message Sequence Chart. Sequence diagrams describe how objects interact over the course of time through an exchange of messages. A single sequence diagram often represents the flow of events for a single use case. The sequence diagrams are depicted in Implementation chapter.

Chapter 6 IMPLEMENTATION

The implementation phase of project is the most important phase as it yields the final solution, which solves the problem. The implementation phase involves the actual materialization of the ideas, which are expressed in the analysis document and developed in the design phase. Implementation should be perfect mapping of the design document in a suitable programming language in order to achieve the necessary final product. Often the products are not what customers want due to incorrect programming language chosen for implementation or unsuitable method of programming. It is better for the coding phase to be directly linked to the design phase in the sense if the design is in terms of object oriented terms then implementation should be preferably carried out in an object oriented way. The factors concerning the programming language and platform chosen are described in the next couple of sections.

6.1   Implementation Requirements

Implementation of any software is always preceded by important decisions regarding selection of the platform, the language used, etc. these decisions are often influenced by several factors such as real environment in which the system works, the speed that is required and other implementation specific details. There are two major implementation decisions that have been made before the implementation of this project. They are as follows:

1. Selection of the programming language for development of the application
2. The development platform chosen is Windows 7(64 bit), Eclipse Indigo 3.7.2, JDK/JRE 1.6.34.

Software Requirement:

•   The language chosen for this project is Java.
•   Operating System used: The Tool will work on all the platforms for which JDK and JRE are available and for which Eclipse version is available.

6.2   Selection of the Platform

The project chose Windows 7 Ultimate for development as Windows 8 is still new.JDK/JRE 1.6.34 is chosen for the project as they are stable. Eclipse Juno(4.2) is still being evaluated by users all over the world. Hence the project decided to go ahead with Indio 3.7.2.

6.3   Selection of Language

For the implementation of project Java was chosen as the existing code was in Java. Java offers myriad advantages as briefed in the section below.

6.4   Implementation Details

6.4.1 Class Diagrams

The Class diagram below depicts the relation between newly introduced classes as part of this project. The inheritance and association of the classes is as shown in the diagram.

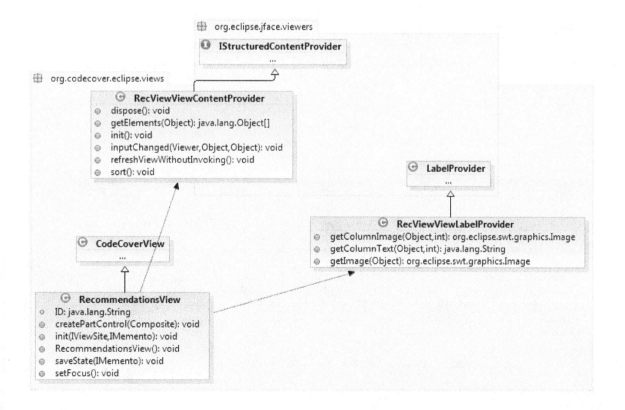

Figure 3. Class Diagrams

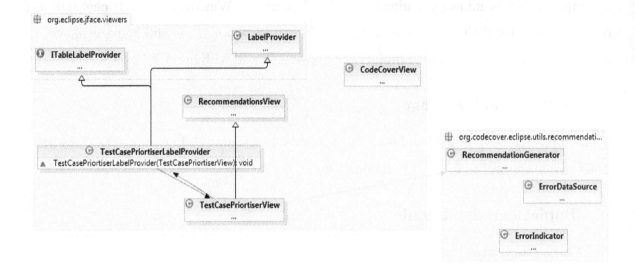

Figure 4. Class Digram of RecommendationGenerator

6.4.2 Package Diagrams

6.4.2.1 RecommendationGenerator package overview.

The diagram below depicts the main package overview. The individual classes in the package are as shown in the diagram.

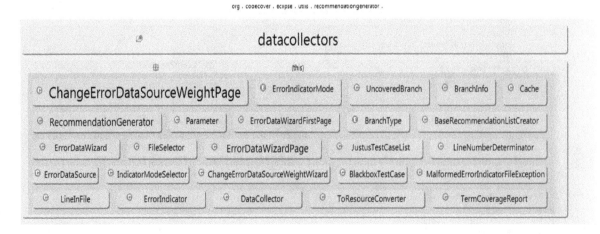

Figure 5. Recommendation Generator Package view

6.4.2.2 Data collectors package overview

Data collector package is as shown below. The individual classes are named as shown in the boxes.

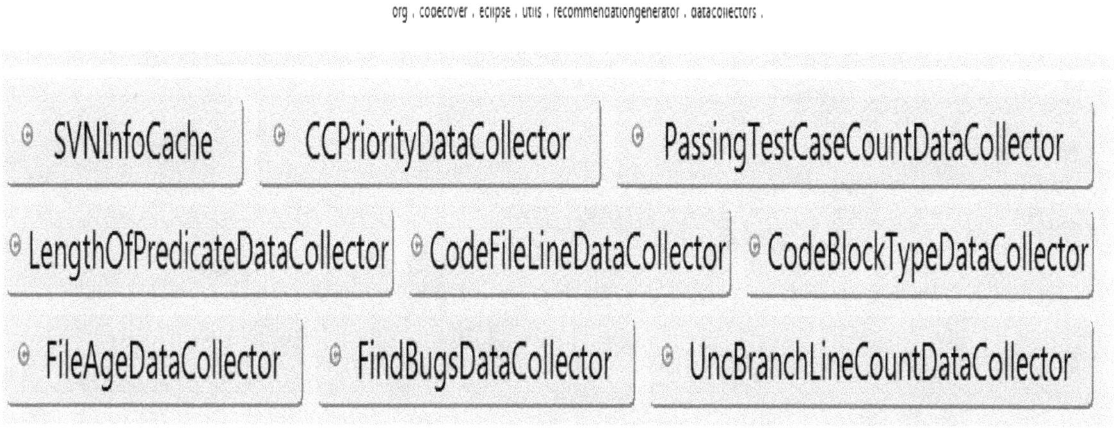

org . codecover . eclipse . utils . recommendationgenerator . datacollectors .

⊙ SVNInfoCache	⊙ CCPriorityDataCollector	⊙ PassingTestCaseCountDataCollector
⊙ LengthOfPredicateDataCollector	⊙ CodeFileLineDataCollector	⊙ CodeBlockTypeDataCollector
⊙ FileAgeDataCollector	⊙ FindBugsDataCollector	⊙ UncBranchLineCountDataCollector

Figure 6. Data Collectors Package overview

6.4.3 Call Flow Diagrams

This section shows the Call flow diagrams.

6.4.3.1 Call Flow High Level

The diagram below shows the high level call flow. This diagram depicts the code level call flow for various classes depicted in the diagram below.

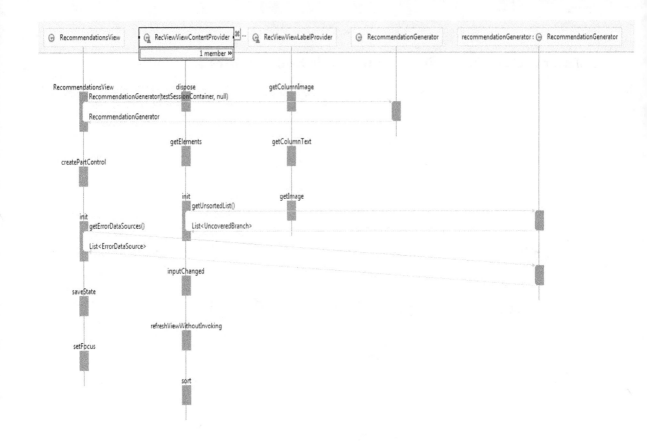

Figure 7. High Level Call Flow

6.4.3.2 Call Flow Recommendation View.

This section is for Call flow when the RecommendationsView class is studied.

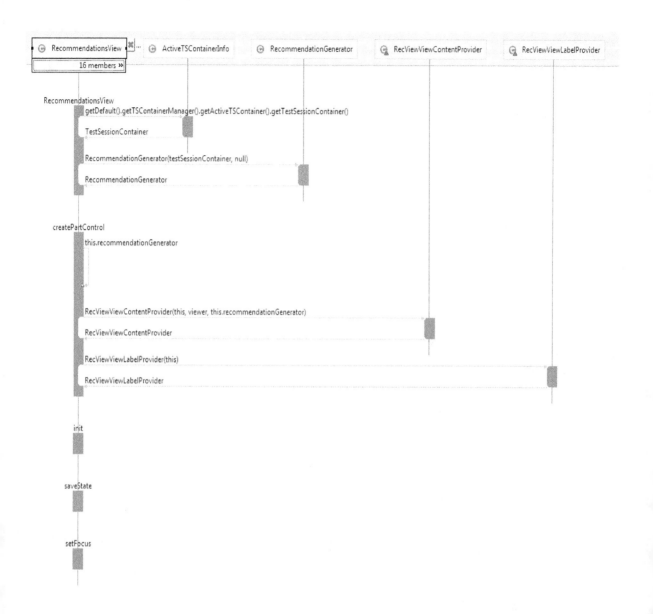

Figure 8. Call Flow Recommendation View

6.4.3.2 Call Flow RecommendationView View Content Provider

The diagram below depicts the RecViewViewContent provider call flow.

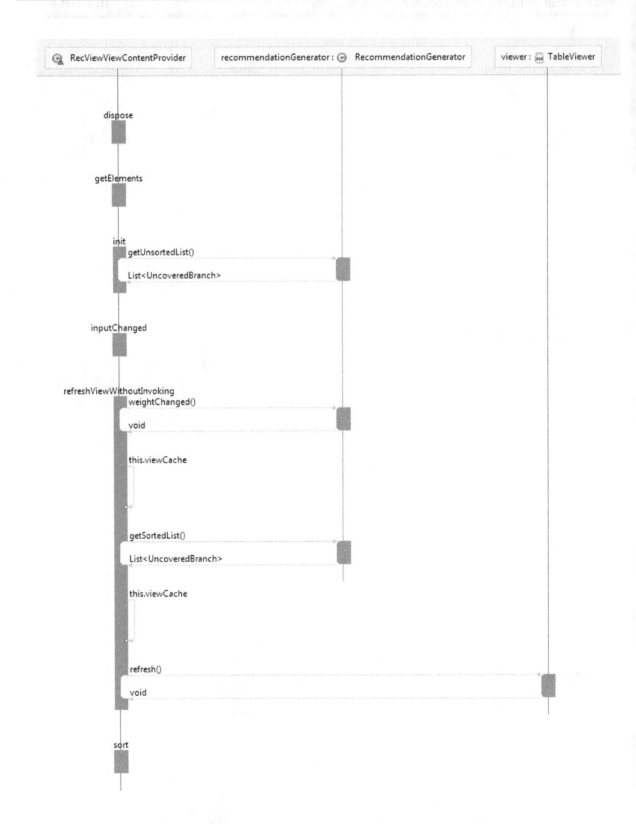

Figure 9. Call Flow RecommendationView View Content Provider

6.4.3.2 Call Flow RecommendationView View Label Provider

The diagram below depicts the RecViewViewLabelProvider related call flow.

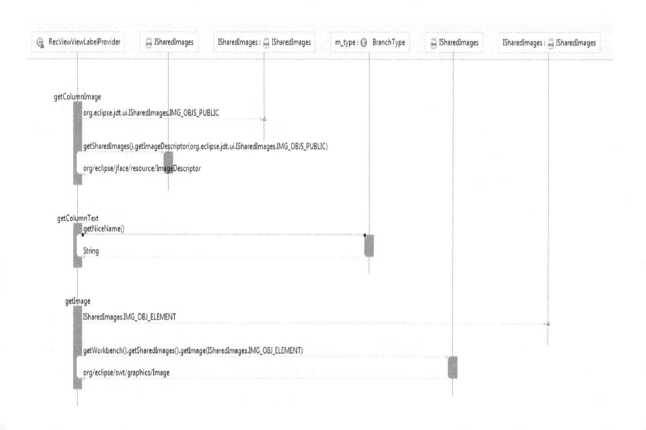

Figure 10. Call Flow RecommendationView View Label Provider

Chapter 7 TESTING

The aim of testing stage is to discover defects/errors by testing individual program components. These components may be functions, objects or modules. During system testing, these components are integrated to form the complete system. At this stage, testing should focus on establishing that the system meets its functional requirements, and does not behave in unexpected ways. Test data are inputs which have been devised to test the system whereas test cases are inputs to test the system and the outputs are predicted from these inputs if the system operates according to its specification. This is to examine the behavior in a cohesive system. The test cases are selected to ensure that the system behavior can be examined in all possible combinations of conditions. Detecting all the different failure modes for software is generally infeasible. Software testing is used in association with verification and validation:

- **Verification:** Have we built the software right (i.e., does it match the specification)?

- **Validation:** Have we built the right software (i.e., is this what the customer wants)?

Testing Process

Testing is an integral part of software development. Testing process, in a way certifies, whether the product, that is developed, complies with the standards, that it was designed to. Testing process involves building of test cases, against which, the product has to be tested. In some cases, test cases are done based on the system requirements specified for the product/software, which is to be developed.

Testing Objectives

These following objectives imply a dramatic change in view port. Testing cannot show the absence of defects, it can only show that software errors are present.

- Testing is process of executing a program with the intent of finding an error.
- A good test case design is one that has a probability of finding an error yet undiscovered.
- A successful test discovers all bugs and user can undertake steps to rectify them.

Testing mainly includes the major activities

- Unit testing
- Integration testing

- System testing

7.1   Test Environment

The software was tested on the following platform.

- Operating System – Windows 7 (64 bit)
- Eclipse Indigo -3.7.2
- Java Development Kit 6

- Apache Ant 1.8.3

7.2   Unit testing

Unit testing is the process of testing individual components in the system. This is a defect testing process so its goal is to expose faults in these components. There are different types of component that may be tested at this stage. Individual functions or methods are the simplest type of component and our tests are a set of calls to these routines with different parameters. All the independent paths were exercised to ensure that all the statements in the module are executed at least once and all the error handling paths were tested. At the end of this testing phase, each unit is found to be working satisfactorily, as regard to the expected output from the module.

7.2.1 Unit Test cases

1 Code Coverage Data Gathering.

Sl No. of Test Case	UT- 1
Name of Test	Code Coverage Data Gathering
Feature being Tested	Code Coverage Data Gathering
Sample Input	Import the component being tested into Eclipse
Expected output	The required code coverage data is generated.

Actual output	The required code coverage data is generated.
Remarks	Pass

Table 7.1 Code Coverage Data Gathering Test Case.

2 Start the recommendation view.

Sl No. of Test Case	UT- 2
Name of Test	Start the Recommendation View.
Feature being Tested	Recommendation View
Sample Input	Component being tested.
Expected output	Recommendation view with populated data.
Actual output	Recommendation view with populated data.
Remarks	Pass

Table 7.2 Recommendation View Start Test Case.

3 Check the Code and CC-Test Columns of the recommendation view population.

Sl No. of Test Case	UT- 3
Name of Test	Code and CC-Test columns of the recommendation view test
Feature being Tested	Code and CC-Test column population in recommendation view
Sample Input	Component being tested.
Expected output	Code and CC-Test columns are populated correctly.

Actual output	Code and CC-Test columns are populated correctly.
Remarks	Pass

Table 7.3 Code and CC-Test columns population Test Case.

4 Check the version history columns of the recommendation view

Sl No. of Test Case	UT- 4
Name of Test	Populate the version history column of recommendation generator
Feature being Tested	Version history column population.
Sample Input	XML with valid data for the version history.
Expected output	Version history is populated correctly.
Actual output	Version history is populated correctly.
Remarks	Pass

Table 7.4 History column population Test Case.

5 Check the population of Expertise columns of the recommendation view

Sl No. of Test Case	UT- 5
Name of Test	Population of expertise column of the recommendation view.
Feature being Tested	Population of the expertise column of the recommendation view.
Sample Input	XML with valid data for expertise.

Expected output	Recommendation view with populated data.
Actual output	Recommendation view with populated data.
Remarks	Pass

Table 7.5 Expertise column population Test Case.

6 Check the population of process related Columns of the recommendation view

Sl No. of Test Case	UT- 6
Name of Test	Populate the process related data column in the recommendation view
Feature being Tested	Population of process related data column in the recommendation view
Sample Input	XML with valid data for the process related information.
Expected output	Recommendation view with populated data.
Actual output	Recommendation view with populated data.
Remarks	Pass

Table 7.6 Process Related Column Population Test Case.

7 Check the quality related columns of the recommendation view

Sl No. of Test Case	UT- 7
Name of Test	Populate the quality related data in the recommendation view
Feature being Tested	Population of quality related data in the recommendation view

Sample Input	XML with valid data for the quality related parameters.
Expected output	Recommendation view with populated data.
Actual output	Recommendation view with populated data.
Remarks	Pass

Table 7.7 Quality Related Column Population Test Case.

8 Check the recommendation view computation.

Sl No. of Test Case	UT- 8
Name of Test	Recommendation View computation.
Feature being Tested	Recommendation View computation.
Sample Input	XMLs for all the columns.
Expected output	Recommendation view with populated data.
Actual output	Recommendation view with populated data.
Remarks	Pass

Table 7.8 Recommendation View Computation Test Case.

9 Check the exporting functionality of recommendation view

Sl No. of Test Case	UT- 9
Name of Test	Exporting the data generated by recommendation view to csv format.

Feature being Tested	Data export.
Sample Input	XMLs with valid data.
Expected output	The generated data is exported to csv format which can be opened in Excel sheet.
Actual output	The generated data is exported to csv format which can be opened in Excel sheet.
Remarks	Pass

Table 7.9 Recommendation View Export Functionality Test Case.

7.3 Integration Testing

Integration testing is another aspect of testing that is generally done in order to uncover errors associated with the flow of data across interfaces. The unit-tested modules are grouped together and tested in small segment, which makes it easier to isolate and correct errors. This approach is continued until all modules are integrated to form the system as a whole.

Please refer Appendix A for more details about build XMLs written for the project.

7.4 System Testing

System testing is actually a series of different tests whose primary purpose is to fully exercise the computer-software based system. The following are the types of system tests that were carried out for the system.

ACTUAL SNAPSHOTS OF THE TOOL OUTPUT POST ENHANCEMENT

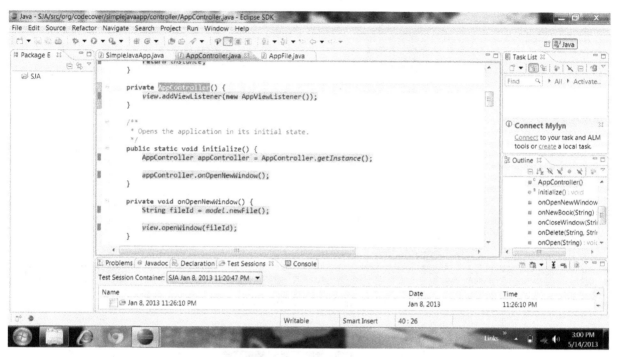

Figure 11. Gathered Coverage Data

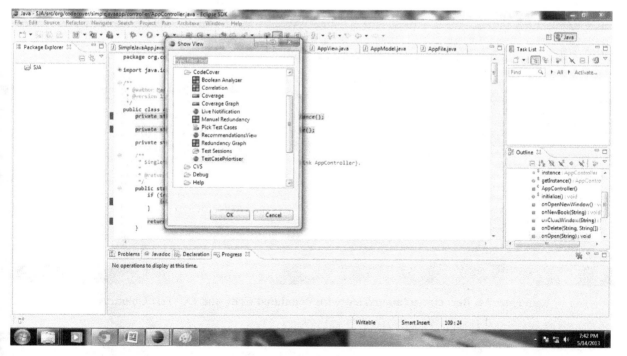

Figure 12. Recommendation View is Added to the List of Views

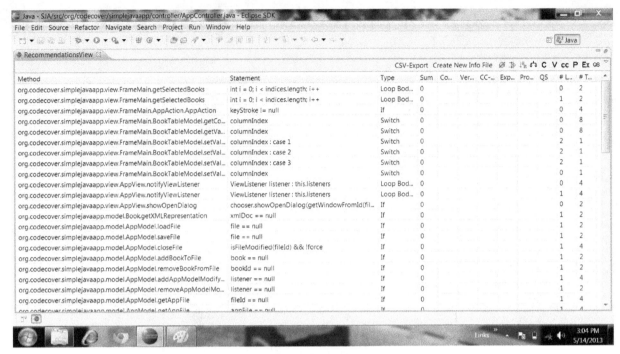

Figure 13. Default Recommendation View

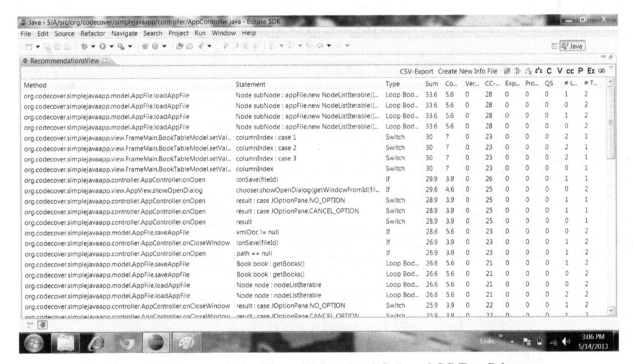

Figure 14. Recommendation View with Populated Code and CC-Test Columns

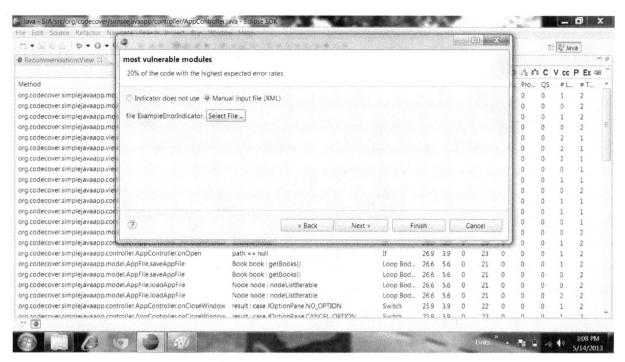

Figure 15. Population of the Data for One of the Columns of Recommendation View

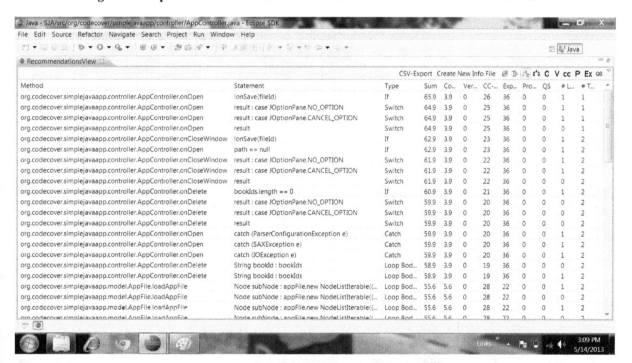

Figure 16. Recommendation View Re-priortization Post Population

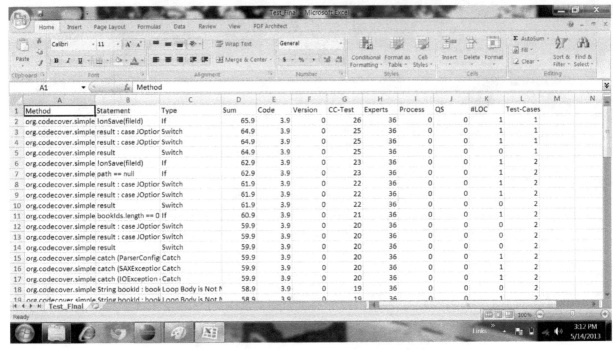

Figure 17. Data Exported to Excel Sheet

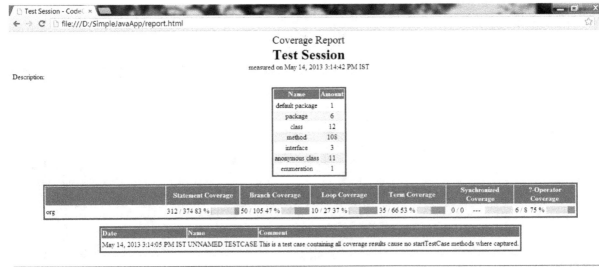

Figure 18. Data Gathered using Ant Build File

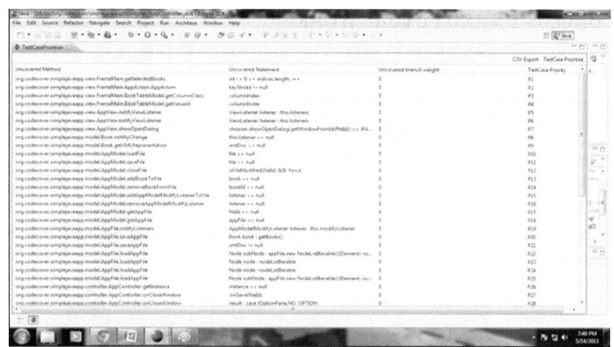

Figure 19. Test Case Prioritizer Before Population

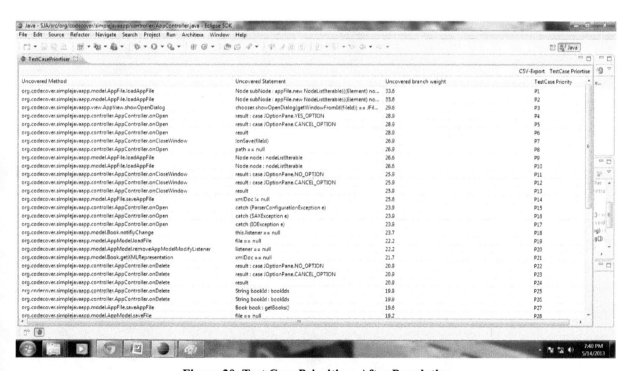

Figure 20. Test Case Prioritizer After Population

CONCLUSION AND FUTURE WORK

This project highlights the strength of Code Coverage Tool called CodeCover. The intended enhancements to the Tool are achieved as part of the Project. The project introduces new functionality called recommendation generator, which recommends test cases on the basis of various input parameters. The recommended test cases help in test suite reduction, Pruning, Augmentation and Consolidation.

The tool can be further strengthened to give static code complexity of the product. Further, tool can think of supporting features such as simple path coverage and data flow coverage.

REFERENCES

[1] CodeCover Home Page=http://codecover.org/.

[2] CodeCover documentation Page=http://codecover.org/documentation/index.html

[3] Cobertura Home Page=http://cobertura.sourceforge.net/.

[4] Emma Home Page=http://emma.sourceforge.net/.

[5] Junit Home Page=http://www.junit.org/.

[6] JavaCodeCoverage Home Page=https://sites.google.com/site/atulkg/resources.

[7] BCEL=http://commons.apache.org/bcel/.

[8] Clover Home Page=http://www.atlassian.com/clover

[9] Jakarta Regexp Package=http://jakarta.apache.org/regexp/.

[10] Eclemma Page=http://www.eclemma.org/

[11] Raghu Lingampally, Atul Gupta and Pankaj Jalote. A Multipurpose Code Coverage Tool for Java in Proceedings of the 40th Hawaii International Conference on System Sciences-2007. IEEE Computer Society.

[12] H. Agrawal, J.R Horgan, E. W Krauser and S. London. Incremental Regression Testing. In ICSM 93: Proceedings of the International Conference on Software Maintenance, IEEE Computer Society.

[13] S. Elbaum, A. G. Malishevsky, and G. Rothermel. Test case prioritization: A family of empirical studies. IEEE Trans.

[14] M. J. Harrold, J. A. Jones, T. Li, D. Liang, A. Orso, M. Pennings, S. Sinha, S. A. Spoon, and A. Gujarathi. Regression test selection for java software. In OOPSLA '01: Proceedings of the 16th ACM SIGPLAN conference on Object Oriented Programming, Systems, Languages, and Applications,pages 312–326, New York, NY, USA, 2001. ACM Press.

[15] J. A. Jones and M. J. Harrold. Test-suite reduction and prioritization for modified condition/decision coverage. IEEE Trans. Softw. Eng., 2003.

[16] M. Lyu, J. Horgan, and S. London. A coverage analysis tool for the effectiveness of software testing. IEEE Trans. on Reliability, 1994.

[17] G. Rothermel, M. J. Harrold, J. Ostrin, and C. Hong. An empirical study of the effects of minimization on the fault detection capabilities of test suites. In ICSM '98: Proceedings of the International Conference on Software Maintenance,Washington, DC, USA, 1998. IEEE Computer Society.

[18] A. Srivastava and J. Thiagarajan. Effectively prioritizing tests in development environment. In ISSTA '02: Proceedings of the 2002 ACM SIGSOFT International Symposium on Software Testing and Analysis, pages 97–106, New York,NY, USA, 2002. ACM Press.

[19] V. Vipindeep and P. Jalote. Efficient static analysis with path pruning using coverage data. In WODA '05: Proceedings of the 3rd Workshop on Dynamic analysis, pages 1–6, New York, NY, USA, 2005. ACM Press.

[20] Misurda J,Clause J.A. Demand-driven structural testing with dynamic instrumentation. In Software Engineering, 2005. ICSE 2005. Proceedings. 27th International Conference. IEEE Conference Publications.

[21] Williams. T. W and Mercer. M.R. Code Coverage, what does it mean in terms of quality. IEEE Conference Publications 2001.

[22] Sakamoto. K and Washizaki H. Open Code Coverage Framework: A Consistent and Flexible Framework for Measuring Test Coverage Supporting Multiple Programming Languages. IEEE Conference Publications 2010.

[23] Adler. Y and Behar. N. Code Coverage Analysis In Practice for Large Systems. IEEE Conference Publications 2011.

[24] Del Frate. F and Grag. P. On the correlation between code coverage and software reliability. IEEE Conference Publications 1995.

[25] Berner. S and Weber. R. Enhancing Software Testing by Judicious Use of Code Coverage Information. IEEE Conference Publications 2007.

[26] Lawrence. J and Clarke. S. How well do professional developers test with code coverage visualizations? An empirical study. IEEE Conference Publications

[27] Wong. W. E and Yu Qi. Effective Fault Localization using Code Coverage. IEEE Conference Publications 2007

[28] Karcich. R. M and Skibbe. R. On software reliability and code coverage. IEEE Conference Publications 1996.

[29]   Mauro Pezze and Michal young. Software Testing and Analysis: Process,Principles, and Techniques. Chapter 14 Structural Testing.

[30] Code Cover Detailed Design Page=http://codecover.org/development/Design.pdf

[31]   Code   Cover   in   Command line=http://codecover.org/documentation/tutorials/how_to_batch.html

[32]   CodeCover   Ant integration=http://codecover.org/documentation/tutorials/ant_manual.html

[33]   CoffeeMaker= http://agile.csc.ncsu.edu/SEMaterials/tutorials/coffee_maker/

[34]   CodeCover Installation=http://codecover.org/documentation/install.html

[35]   Metrics Plug in For Eclipse= http://metrics.sourceforge.net/.

[36]   CodeCover detailed design http://codecover.org/development/Design.pdf

[37]   Hong Mei and Dan Hao. A Static approach to prioritizing Junit Test cases.IEEE transactions 2012.

[38]   Bluemke, I.; Rembiszewski, A. Dataflow Approach to Testing Java Programs. IEEE conferences 2009.

[39]   Li, J.J.; Horgan, J.R. A tool suite for diagnosis and testing of software design specifications. IEEE conference publications 2000.

[40]   Van Rompaey, B.; Demeyer, S.Estimation of Test Code Changes Using Historical Release Data.IEEE conference publication 2008.

[41]   Williams, T.W.; Mercer, M.R.; Mucha, J.P.; Kapur, R.Code coverage, what does it mean in terms of quality?.IEEE conference publications 2001.

[42]   Sanguinetti, J.; Zhang, E. The relationship of code coverage metrics on high-level and RTL code.IEEE conference publications 2010.

[43]   Li, J.J. Prioritize code for testing to improve code coverage of complex software. IEEE conference publications 2005/

[44]   Elbaum, S.; Gable, D.; Rothermel, G.The impact of software evolution on code coverage information. IEEE conference publications 2001.

[45]   Minakova, K.; Reinsalu, U.; Chepurov, A.; Raik, J.; Jenihhin, M.; Ubar, R. High-level decision diagram manipulations for code coverage analysis. IEEE Conference publications 2008.

[46]   Del Frate, F.; Garg, P.; Mathur, A.P.; Pasquini, A. On the correlation between code coverage and software reliability. IEEE conference publications 1995.

APPENDIX A

XML files for builds for Integration testing.

1 Integration testing with Ant build file.

The build.xml looks as follows:

```xml
<project default="create-report">
<property name="codecoverDir"
value="D:\Test_Ant\Test_Ant\trunk\code\release"/>
<property name="sourceDir" value="src"/>
<property name="instrumentedSourceDir" value="instrumented"/>
<property name="mainClassName"
value="org.codecover.simplejavaapp.SimpleJavaApp"/>
<taskdef name="codecover" classname="org.codecover.ant.CodecoverTask"
classpath="${codecoverDir}/lib/codecover-ant.jar"/>
<target name="clean">
<delete>
<fileset dir="." includes="*.clf"/>
</delete>
<delete file="codecover.xml"/>
<delete file="report.html"/>
<delete dir="report.html-files"/>
</target>
<target name="instrument-sources" depends="clean">
<codecover>
<instrument containerId="c" language="java"
destination="${instrumentedSourceDir}" charset="utf-8"
copyUninstrumented="yes">
<source dir="${sourceDir}">
<include name="**/*.java"/>
</source>
</instrument>
<save containerId="c" filename="codecover.xml"/>
</codecover>
</target>
<target name="compile-instrumented" depends="instrument-sources">
<javac srcdir="${instrumentedSourceDir}"
destdir="${instrumentedSourceDir}" encoding="utf-8" target="1.5"
debug="true" classpath="${codecoverDir}/lib/codecover-instrumentation-
java.jar" includeAntRuntime="false"></javac>
</target>
<target name="run-instrumented" depends="compile-instrumented">
<java classpath="${instrumentedSourceDir}:${codecoverDir}/lib/codecover-
instrumentation-java.jar" fork="true" failonerror="true"
classname="${mainClassName}">
```

```
<jvmarg value="-Dorg.codecover.coverage-log-file=test.clf"/>
</java>
</target>
<target name="create-report" depends="run-instrumented">
<codecover>
<load containerId="c" filename="codecover.xml"/>
<analyze containerId="c" coverageLog="test.clf" name="Test Session"/>
<save containerId="c" filename="codecover.xml"/>
<report containerId="c" destination="report.html"
template="${codecoverDir}/report-templates/HTML_Report_hierarchic.xml">
<testCases>
<testSession pattern=".*">
<testCase pattern=".*"/>
</testSession>
</testCases>
</report>
</codecover>
</target>
</project>
```

2 Integration testing with Ant build file with Junit test cases.

The build.xml looks as follows:

```
<project default="create-report">
<property name="codecoverDir"
value="D:\Test_Ant\Test_Ant\trunk\code\release"/>
<property name="sourceDir" value="src"/>
<property name="testDir" value="unittests"/>
<property name="instrumentedSourceDir" value="instrumented"/>
<property name="mainClassName" value="edu.ncsu.csc326.coffeemaker.Main"/>
<property name="master-test-suite"
value="edu.ncsu.csc326.coffeemaker.CoffeeMakerTest"/>
<taskdef name="codecover" classname="org.codecover.ant.CodecoverTask"
classpath="${codecoverDir}/lib/codecover-ant.jar"/>
<target name="clean">
<delete>
<fileset dir="." includes="*.clf"/>
</delete>
<delete file="codecover.xml"/>
<delete file="report.html"/>
<delete dir="report.html-files"/>
</target>


<target name="instrument-sources" depends="clean">
<codecover>
```

```xml
<instrument containerId="c" language="java"
destination="${instrumentedSourceDir}" charset="utf-8"
copyUninstrumented="yes">
<source dir="${sourceDir}">
<include name="**/*.java"/>
</source>
</instrument>
<save containerId="c" filename="codecover.xml"/>
</codecover>
</target>




<target name="collect">
  <copy todir="${instrumentedSourceDir}">
    <fileset dir="${testDir}" />
    <include name="**/*.java"/>
  </copy>
</target>




<target name="compile-instrumented" depends="instrument-sources">
<javac srcdir="${instrumentedSourceDir}"
destdir="${instrumentedSourceDir}" encoding="utf-8" target="1.5"
debug="true" classpath="C:\Users\Abhinandan\Desktop\junit4.9\junit-
4.9.jar" includeAntRuntime="false"/>
</target>




<target name="run-instrumented" depends="compile-instrumented">
<java fork="true" classname="org.codecover.junit4.core.TestRunner">
<classpath>
<!-- code cover jars -->
<pathelement location="D:\junit4.9\junit-4.9.jar"/>
<pathelement location="${codecoverDir}/lib/JUnit-TestRunner.jar"/>
<pathelement location="${codecoverDir}/lib/codecover-ant.jar"/>
<pathelement location="${codecoverDir}/lib/codecover-batch.jar"/>
<pathelement location="${codecoverDir}/lib/codecover-core.jar"/>
<pathelement path="${instrumentedSourceDir}"/>
</classpath>
<jvmarg value="-Dorg.codecover.coverage-log-file=test.clf"/>
<arg value="${master-test-suite}"/>
</java>
</target>
<target name="create-report" depends="run-instrumented">
<codecover>
<load containerId="c" filename="codecover.xml"/>
```

```
<analyze containerId="c" coverageLog="test.clf" name="Test Session"/>
<save containerId="c" filename="codecover.xml"/>
<report containerId="c" destination="report.html"
template="${codecoverDir}/report-templates/HTML_Report_hierarchic.xml">
<testCases>
<testSession pattern=".*">
<testCase pattern=".*"/>
</testSession>
</testCases>
</report>
</codecover>
</target>
</project>
```